Autumntime in the Forest

EDWARD ALAN KURTZ

Audiobook

Print • eBook • Audiobook

Copyright © 2016 Edward Alan Kurtz
Published by Stergiou Limited
All rights reserved.

Copyright
Autumntime in the Forest
2016 © Edward Alan Kurtz
Images & Illustrations: Adobe Stock
Cover image: © Annamei | Adobe Stock

Available in print, eBook and audiobook

ISBN: 978-1-910370-86-5 (Stergiou Limited-Assigned)
ISBN: 978-1-537486-16-1 (CreateSpace-Assigned)
ePub ISBN: 978-1-910370-87-2 (Stergiou Limited-Assigned)

Published by Stergiou Limited
Suite A, 6 Honduras Street,
London EC1Y 0TH, United Kingdom
Email: admin@stergioultd.com
Web: http://stergioultd.com
All rights reserved

© littleartvector | Adobe Stock

CONTENTS

Chapter One	At the Top of the Old Pine Tree	4
Chapter Two	Teatime	10
Chapter Three	The Pond	16
Chapter Four	Olivia	22
Chapter Five	The Waterfall	28
Chapter Six	A Trip to the Village	34
Chapter Seven	The Meeting	38
Chapter Eight	The Bright Sky	44
Chapter Nine	Buckets!	48
Chapter Ten	Little Green Plants	54
The author	Edward Alan Kurtz	60

© comodo777 | Adobe Stock

CHAPTER ONE

At the Top of the Old Pine Tree

Once upon a time, there was a big and beautiful forest, and in that forest there was a tall, old pine tree. There were many areas that made up this big forest: there were hills and valleys; there were rivers and streams and a lake; there were areas that were thick with trees, and other areas that opened into meadows with grass and wildflowers.

And there were animals, of course! Lots of animals. There was a group of beavers that had built a dam for their houses, and this had created the lake that was not too far away from the old pine tree.

There were caves along one of the ridges, and in this cave, a mother bear was raising her two cubs. Along the top of another ridge, there lived a group of vultures. They were not the most popular animals in the forest, so many of the other animals stayed away from the place where the vultures lived.

There were many deer that lived near the meadows; they quietly came out of the forest sometimes to find things to eat in the meadows. The grasses were good, and some of the wildflowers were extra tasty to the deer.

The deer, like so many of the other animals in the forest, often paid a visit to the big old pine tree. It was a special and magical place. The pine tree had dropped some of its needles to the ground below, and this made a very soft place for animals to rest.

And because of the shade that it created, the area at the bottom of the old pine tree was a favourite place for animals to rest in the summertime when the weather was hot and sunny.

This pine tree also played another important role in the life of the forest and the lives of the animals. For it was here that all of the animals gathered if there was a problem in the forest. It was a meeting place where they could all talk and try to come up with a way to fix the problem.

There was one more thing about the pine tree that made it special: it was the home of three birds and one squirrel. They all lived high up in the pine tree and they were very good friends.

Who were these animals and how did they become such good friends?

There were three birds who lived in houses almost at the very top of the pine tree.

Wendy the Warbler

Wally the Woodlark

© cat_arch_angel | Adobe Stock

© Gennadij Kurilin | Adobe Stock

They were Wendy the Warbler, Wally the Woodlark, and William the Woodpecker. Sebastian the Squirrel was the fourth friend, and he lived just a couple of branches below where the three birds lived.

The four friends had known each other for a long time. And then, one day, they had decided to build their houses at the top of the old pine tree.

Each of the four friends had a favourite colour and each one was known by all of the other animals in the forest as being special.

Wendy was known for being a very smart bird. She was also helpful, so she had often come to the rescue when the forest animals faced a problem.

Her favourite colour was pink. The first thing that was pink was her front door, and when you went inside her house, you saw how much she loved the colour pink. Her walls, her rugs, her furniture, the quilt on her bed, her kitchen table and chairs:

William the Woodpecker

Sebastian the Squirrel

everything was pink!

She and her three friends often got together for afternoon tea, so Wendy's tea cups and tea pot were all decorated with pink flowers.

Wally was the second friend. Wally was a good bird, but he was very messy and not at all organized. The other three friends had learned to be patient with Wally. He was always late; he often forgot things; he couldn't find things he was looking for in his house; and he didn't pay attention to the conversation when the four friends got together. He did a lot of day dreaming, and the other three friends often had to call his name and try to bring him back into the conversation.

Wally's favourite colour was blue. Just like Wendy, Wally had painted his front door his favourite colour, so you saw blue even before you knocked on his door. Sometimes Wally answered the knock on his front door, but sometimes his mind was some other place, and he didn't even notice the knocking sound. The other three friends had learned that they had to knock very loudly to get Wally to come to his front door.

His walls and rugs were blue as were the quilt on his bed, his furniture, the slippers that he kept right inside of his front door, his backpack, and his teapot and teacups.

Next there was William. William's house was quite different from Wendy's house and Wally's house. Since William was a woodpecker, he had pecked a hole in the old pine tree to make his front door. He kept on pecking until the area inside the tree was big enough for his house. It was no wonder that William was known for being very active, because it took that kind of animal to do all of that pecking!

His favourite colour was purple, so his front door and everything inside of his house was purple. His favourite reading chair was purple, and next to it stood a lamp with a purple lampshade.

Sebastian's house was like William's house. In fact, William had made Sebastian's house for him. He had to make it bigger than his house, because Sebastian was bigger than William.

Sebastian was known for being nosy: he loved to gossip, so the most important thing in his house was his telephone. It was brown just like everything else in his house. Brown was his favourite colour because it was the colour of his fur.

It was teatime... what were the four friends talking about?

© comodo777 | Adobe Stock

CHAPTER TWO

Teatime

Today, the four friends had met at Wendy's house. This is where they usually met because Wendy loved to prepare afternoon tea, and she was very good at it! The tea was just perfect and the scones were always delicious.

But something was different about today's teatime. When they met for tea, they usually had happy things to talk about. Or maybe someone had some news about one of their other friends. It was often Sebastian who had the most to tell the other three friends because he spent a good part of his day on his brown telephone!

"This is really serious," said William.

"I agree," said Sebastian.

"I think this just might turn out to be the most serious problem we have ever faced here in our forest," said Wendy.

The three friends turned towards Wally to see if he had anything to say, but he was counting the leaves that were flying past Wendy's window.

Wendy wanted Wally to be a part of the conversation, so she asked, "And what do you think about this, Wally?"

"What?" asked Wally. He was suddenly paying attention again to what was going on inside Wendy's house instead of watching the leaves.

"Big River," answered Wendy.

"What about it?" asked Wally.

"Haven't you been listening at all?" asked Sebastian.

"Sorry," answered Wally. "I was watching all of the leaves dropping."

It had been a very dry summer, and many of the trees were losing their leaves because the trees were not getting enough water to drink. The pine tree where they lived was quite tall, but gusts of wind often blew the dry leaves high up into the air before they fell down to the floor of the forest.

"Yes, you're right," said William. "There are lots of leaves out there. But what do you think about Big River?"

"I think someone picked the wrong name when they were thinking about what to call it," answered Wally.

Big River was the river that was closest to the old pine tree. And many of their other friends lived near the river.

"They should have named it 'Little Trickle,'" said Wally.

Wendy frowned. "This is serious and not something to joke about," she said.

"I don't mean to joke about it," said William. "But Wally is just about right. I was there early this morning, and now there are some places where there is no water at all. There are small pools here and there, but anyone can easily walk across to the other side without getting wet!"

"Have you heard about the beavers?" asked Sebastian.

"What are they doing?" asked Wendy.

"The water in their lake is so low now that you can see the doors to their houses," said Sebastian. "As you know the level of water is usually high enough to cover their doors, and they have to swim underwater to get to their front doors."

"That's not good," said Wendy. "Because now any animal can just go right on in to the beavers' front doors."

"They don't know what to do," added Sebastian. "They're thinking they might have to move to another river."

"But where would they go?" asked William. "The next closest river is Raging River, and they can't build a dam there."

"Is there any water in Raging River?" asked Wendy.

"Not right now," answered Sebastian. "But this dry weather is not going to last forever. And so they know it's not a good place to build a dam, because the water will be too dangerous when it finally starts to rain again."

Wendy made more tea and gave some to each of them. She also brought out some more scones.

"I guess there is no point in going up to Big Spring, is there?" she asked as she sat down.

Big Spring was the underground spring upriver. It was the source of the river, where Big River began.

"What could we do up there?" asked Sebastian.

"I don't know," answered Wendy. "It's just that there doesn't seem to be anything we can do, and I was thinking that maybe if we went up to Big Spring and had a look around, we might find something that would help us with this water problem."

"It's worth a try," said William. "Like you said, no one seems to know what to do."

It was too late in the day to start a walk towards Big Spring, so they made plans to leave early the next morning.

"Don't forget your backpacks," said Wendy.

"And some water," added William.

"And a snack," added Sebastian.

The three of them looked over at Wally. He was daydreaming again, so after they got his attention, they explained where they were going and when.

The next morning William knocked loudly on Wally's door to make sure he was up. He was and had his backpack ready to go. Soon they were joined by Wendy. Sebastian was waiting for them at the bottom of the pine tree.

They didn't need Sebastian's map this time, because they had all been to Big Spring many times. They started to walk away from the old pine tree and soon came to what was left of Big River. They followed Big River to the north where Big Spring was found.

As they walked along the river, they saw places where there were still some pools of water, but most of the riverbed was dry. They saw plenty of rocks in the riverbed, but very little water.

They finally arrived at Big Spring. Big Spring was made up of several huge stones that were next to a small hill. It was at the bottom of two or three of these huge stones that the water usually came up out of the ground. It had always flowed fast, and there had always been a lot of water coming up out of the spring, but today there was very little water.

"I guess there's nothing we can do here," said Wendy.

At least they had tried. As they walked back to the pine tree, no one spoke. They were all thinking the same thing: what can we try next?

© comodo777 | Adobe Stock

CHAPTER THREE

The Pond

The four friends walked back to the old pine tree. It had been a long and unhappy day for them, so they said goodnight and returned to their houses for some much-needed sleep.

Wendy was tired, but she did not sleep very well. She woke up many times during the night thinking about the water problem. What could they do?

They couldn't make rain: how do you ask rain clouds to come to where you live and make rain for you? It's not possible.

Their trip to Big Spring had showed them that there was nothing they could do there to make Big River big again.

She was also thinking about Raging River. Was there some way to get some water from Raging River? But then she remembered that Raging River was as empty as Big River.

Come on, Wendy, she said to herself. Think!

There were several things she could think of that might solve their problem.

When they had hiked to the top of Mount Evergreen during the summer, they had stopped at a beautiful waterfall on the way up. Was there any way to get water from that waterfall over to Big River?

She also remembered the big lake they could see when they were at the top of Mount Evergreen. It was very far away, and no one knew anything about it because no one had ever visited it. Was it possible to bring water from that lake the whole way over to Big River?

Were there any rivers or lakes or streams on Sebastian's map? He had bought a map to help them when they hiked to the top of Mount Evergreen during the summer. Wendy thought that maybe, just maybe, there could be some water somewhere not too far away that they could find on Sebastian's map.

She thought for a little while about the people who lived in the nearby village. Could they help? The villagers had become friends with all of the animals in the forest over Christmas when the villagers wanted to chop down the old pine tree for their village Christmas tree. The animals were able to talk the villagers out of chopping down the tree. Instead they all came together to decorate the tree right where it was: in the middle of the forest. But the villagers could not make it rain.

Wendy finally fell asleep. When she woke up, the sun was shining brightly in her bedroom. She had been dreaming about the village and Christmas. In her dream, she saw a white bird flying in and out of the church in the village.

Olivia!

It was Olivia in her dream. Wendy was smart, but Olivia was wise. Everyone in the forest knew her as a very wise owl. She had been the one who had heard the villagers' Christmas plans, and she was the one who helped to save the old pine tree.

Maybe Olivia would have an idea about the water problem. But first, Wendy wanted to have a look at Sebastian's map.

It was shortly after this that she knocked on Wally's door and then William's door and, finally, Sebastian's door. Sebastian invited the three of them to come in.

"Do you still have your map?" asked Wendy. "The one we used when we went up to Mount Evergreen?"

"Yes," said Sebastian. "I keep it right here in the pocket of my backpack. What are you thinking about?" he asked as he pulled out the map and spread it on top of his kitchen table.

"I was just thinking that there might be other places where there is water, and we just don't know about them," said Wendy.

"It's worth a try," said William.

Wally was looking around Sebastian's house and not paying attention, as usual. Wendy nudged him so that he could look at the map with the others.

The old pine tree was quite near the center of the forest, so they started looking on the map at the place where the old pine tree was marked. They could see Big River and the lake the beavers had made; they could see Big Spring, which was the source of Big River; they could see Raging River; and of course, they could see hills and mountains and ridges and valleys.

"What is this?" asked Wendy as she pointed at a small blue area in the opposite direction from the two rivers.

"I don't know," said Sebastian. "Almost everything that is marked has a name written on the map, but this one doesn't."

"It doesn't look like it's very far away," said William.

"You're right," said Wendy. "It looks closer than Big Spring. Anybody want to take another walk?"

So they all packed their backpacks with snacks and Sebastian's map and off they went on yet another adventure.

It was still early in the morning, so it wasn't too hot, especially as they walked under the shade of the trees. But there wasn't as much shade now as there had been during the summer because the trees were dropping their leaves.

"The leaves are not going to be pretty this year," said Wendy. "The trees are losing their leaves because they are so thirsty."

Sebastian held the map in his left hand so that he could use his right hand to point at things they were passing, things that were shown on the map.

The path they were following was leading them through a small valley between two hills. There was a group of evergreen trees on the map and the water they were looking for was just beyond the evergreen trees.

When they had passed these trees, they saw what used to be a pond.

A bird flew above them and said, "All gone. All gone."

The plants around the dried up pond were all dead and brown.

"Well, at least now we know," said Wendy.

CHAPTER FOUR

Olivia

Before returning to the old pine tree, the four friends spent a little time walking around the pond.

"It's so sad," said Wendy. "When the water goes away, the plants and animals go away too."

"Yes," agreed William. "There were probably frogs and birds and maybe even fish here. But now there's nothing."

"This makes it even more important for us to find a way to have water near the old pine tree," said Sebastian.

"You're right," said Wendy. "And the only other thing I can think of is to go and talk to Olivia."

"But she can't make rain," said Sebastian.

"I know," said Wendy. "But she's so wise. Maybe there's something we haven't thought of yet."

They all agreed: it was time to talk to Olivia.

The four friends had a little snack as they sat on some rocks next to what used to be the pond. Then they packed up their backpacks and began the trip back to the old pine tree. Sebastian had tucked his map into one of the pockets of his backpack. He didn't need the map because it was an easy trip and he already knew the way home.

When they reached the old pine tree, they put their backpacks in their houses. Then they continued their trip because Olivia lived in another tree that was across the forest.

Olivia's feathers were white and so this was her favourite colour. Everything inside her house was white including her rugs, so everyone tried hard not to bring any dirt in when they visited Olivia.

When the four friends knocked on Olivia's white door, they were not sure what to expect. Because owls sleep during the day and are active during the night, the four friends always had to wake her up. They didn't like to wake her up from sleeping, but sometimes things were so important that they had to wake her.

"Who? Who? Who?" asked Olivia when they had knocked on her door.

"It's Wendy and Wally and William and Sebastian," answered Wendy.

Finally, she opened her front door. She shaded her eyes from the bright sun.

"We're so sorry we woke you," said Wendy.

"Oh, that's okay," said Olivia. "Please come on in and sit down."

The four friends went inside and Olivia closed the door.

"Would you like some tea?" she asked them.

"That would be great," they all answered.

She prepared the tea and put it in her white teapot. She carried it along with her white cups and saucers to where her visitors were sitting.

As she began to arrange everything on the table, she asked them, "How can I help you?"

She started to pour the tea into the teacups as the four friends explained everything to her: how they wanted to find a way to fix the problem of not having enough water; how Big River and the beaver's lake and Raging River were almost dry; how they had walked to Big Spring and then today to the pond which they also found dried up.

They also told her about their walk to the top of Mount Evergreen and what they had seen: the waterfall and the huge lake.

"Yes, I agree that we have a serious problem here," said Olivia. "But what do you think that I can do?"

"We've tried these other ways," said William. "And nothing is working."

"And you're the smartest animal in the forest," added Wally, who was paying attention because there was tea and scones in front of him.

"Well, that's very nice of you to say that," said Olivia. "Thank you. But I really don't know what to do. It's simply a case of not enough rain, and there's no way I can make it rain."

"Is there any way for us to make more water come up out of Big Spring?" asked Wendy.

"I don't think so," answered Olivia. "The water that flows through Big River above ground flows just like that underground. So if there isn't much water above the ground, you can be pretty sure that there isn't much water flowing underground."

There was a little break in the conversation as they all drank some tea and ate some scones. After a while, Sebastian said, "What about the waterfall on Mount Evergreen? Is there some way to get that water to come over to our area of the forest?"

Olivia thought for a little while and then said, "I think it's possible, but I also think it would be very difficult to do. You would have to dig a canal, and for that you'll get the help of the villagers."

"And the ridges," added Sebastian.

"What ridges?" asked Olivia.

"When we walked to Mount Evergreen, we had to cross two ridges," answered Sebastian. "And because they were high and rocky and dangerous, we had to find ways around them."

"That makes it sound almost impossible to build a canal," said Olivia.

"And we don't know if the waterfall is still flowing, or if it has become like the rivers and dried up," said Wendy.

"Even if it is still flowing, digging a canal would take a really long time, especially with those two ridges," said Olivia.

There was more silence as they all thought about the problem.

Suddenly, William said, "What about a raised canal?"

Everyone looked at him because they didn't understand what he meant.

"We could build long wooden boxes and connect them," said William. "And they

"Hmm," said Olivia. "That's an interesting idea. It would be a raised wooden canal or channel starting up at the waterfall and slowly making its way across the tops of the ridges down here to our part of the forest. And you would need to seal the wood so that the water would not drip out of the channel."

"So what should we do?" asked Wendy.

"I think you need to do two things," answered Olivia. "You need to find out if the waterfall is still flowing. And you need to ask the villagers if they will help you."

© comodo777 | Adobe Stock

CHAPTER FIVE

The Waterfall

The four friends thanked Olivia for her help and her tea, and then they said goodbye. They walked back to the old pine tree. As they walked, they made plans to go back to the waterfall on Mount Evergreen.

First, they stopped at Cherry the Chipmunk's house. They were going to invite her to go along on their trip because she had joined them in the summertime. But she was not at home. One of her neighbors said Cherry was visiting her cousin in another part of the forest.

So it was just going to be the four of them. They each packed their backpacks that evening and went to sleep early. They left early in the morning because they did not want to spend the night camping at the top of Mount Evergreen. So they were going to try to go faster this time and return in the evening. One thing that they each made sure they packed was a torch.

The four friends left the old pine tree before the sun came up. They knew their way around this part of the forest, so close to the pine tree, and there was a full moon, so they didn't need their torches yet.

The sun started to peep through the forest towards the east. They had already passed Big River and were now walking along Ridley's Ridge.

The last time they had passed by here, a huge rock had rolled down, and Wally had been trapped underneath it. So this year, the four friends knew that they had to leave the path and go around the fallen rock. Then they got back on the path and continued. The vultures that sat up at the top of the ridge didn't even bother to get out their white napkins for dinner; they could see that the four friends already knew how to avoid the dangerous rocks.

After leaving Ridley's Ridge, the four friends started to get close to Raging River. They did not hear it like last time because now it was so empty. In fact, they didn't need to look for the bridge they had made to cross Raging River in the summertime; there was so little water this time that they could just walk across the river.

After crossing Raging River, they continued through the forest until they came to the meadow they had discovered the last time. They were shocked!

"I can't believe this is the same meadow," said William.

"There are no wildflowers anywhere," added Wendy.

"And all of the grass is brown and dry," said Sebastian.

"And no deer this time," added Wally.

The last time, they had seen some deer far across on the other side of the meadow. It had been green and full of beautiful wildflowers. But with no water, everything had turned brown. They were sad to see the meadow look like this, but they continued on their way.

Soon, they came to Runyon Ridge. They quietly walked past the first cave they came to because this cave had been used by a mother bear and her two cubs. They didn't know if the mother bear and her cubs were still around. It had been a dangerous situation, so they walked quickly and quietly because they didn't want to meet the mother bear again.

They continued until they came to the second cave. This was the correct cave; this was the tunnel that led them under Runyon Ridge to the next valley where Mount Evergreen was. As they went through the cave, they saw the bats again, and they stopped to look at the strange glowworms for a short time.

They came out of the cave and started to walk up the path that led to the top of Mount Evergreen. They didn't stop to rest as they started to go up the path, because it was already midday.

"I think we're getting close to the waterfall," said Sebastian. "It's marked here on the map."

"Yes," added Wendy. "I kind of remember this part of our trip and I remember the waterfall was not too much further."

They were wrong. There was no waterfall!

They stood and looked at the bare rock where the water had fallen down, and at the empty pool that had been so beautiful last year surrounded by green ferns. There were no ferns, no pool, and no waterfall.

"I can't believe this," said William.

The four of them just stood there: they were so shocked and sad at the same time. They sat down and had a little snack and a little rest.

As they were sitting on the rocks that surrounded the dry pool, they noticed a little frog sitting nearby.

"Hello, little frog," said Wendy.

"Hello," said the frog.

"We came from the old pine tree looking for water," said William. "We thought there might be some in this waterfall."

"No water on the mountain," croaked the old frog. "Everyone's gone."

"When did the water stop?" asked Sebastian.

"Hmm," answered the frog. "My memory's not so good any more, but I would say at least two weeks ago."

"Do you happen to know if there is any water still left in the big lake on the other side of the mountain?" asked Wendy.

"No lake," answered the old frog. "All gone."

The four friends thanked the old frog and he slowly walked over to a tiny puddle of water that was all that was left of the pool at the foot of the waterfall.

"This is really bad news," said William.

"It is," said Wendy. "There's nothing else we can do."

"We better get started back home," said Sebastian.

They found Wally drawing in the dry mud with a stick.

"Let's go, Wally," they said.

They went back the same way: Runyon Ridge, the meadow, Raging River, Ridley Ridge, and along Big River.

The four friends were sad as they said goodnight to each other. Maybe someone would think of a new idea.

CHAPTER SIX

A Trip to the Village

Wendy was up early again before the sun came up. She decided to go to Olivia's house to let her know what the four friends had discovered yesterday. Wendy knocked on Olivia's front door: there was no answer, so Wendy knew she was a little early, and she had to wait for Olivia to return home.

This was a good time to visit Olivia because she was usually just coming back home from her nighttime activities, and she hadn't gone to bed yet.

Wendy looked up into the skies and saw lots of stars but no white feathers. Finally, she saw Olivia in the distance flying silently towards her house.

As she landed on the branch outside her front door, Olivia said, "Well, hello, Wendy. Come on in and tell me all about your trip yesterday."

They went inside and sat down.

"It's not good news, I'm afraid," said Wendy. "The waterfall and the pool below it are both dry."

"I'm not surprised to hear you tell me this," said Olivia. "In fact, I would have been very surprised if you had come back home and told me there was still water over there."

"Why?" asked Wendy.

"Because this is the longest anyone can remember that we've not had rain," answered Olivia. "About ten years ago, we had a similar situation, but it was not nearly as bad as this year."

The two birds were quiet for a while. Olivia had made a pot of tea, and now, she and Wendy were both sipping the tea out of Olivia's beautiful white teacups.

Finally Wendy spoke: "I understand that there must be clouds in the sky for there to be rain."

"Yes, that's right," said Olivia.

"But where are the clouds?" asked Wendy. "Where have all of the clouds gone?"

"That is a good question," answered Olivia. "Usually, we have times when there are no clouds, and then these times are followed by times when we have clouds. Sometimes, the clouds make rain for us, and sometimes, they just pass by in the wind."

Wendy sipped her tea and thought for a while.

"And does anyone know why there have been no clouds for such a long time?" asked Wendy. "I mean: not only are there not clouds that bring us rain, but there are also no clouds that pass by without making rain."

"Another good question," answered Olivia. "I'm afraid I don't have a good answer. I do know that there are many things that cause the weather to be one way or another. For example, if there is a storm at sea, sometimes it comes in towards the land and brings rain with it."

"But we're not close to the sea," said Wendy.

"You're right, of course," said Olivia. "I was just using that as one example. But the point is that the weather in one area can cause the weather in another area to change. And the second point is that we can't control the weather; we just have to wait."

Suddenly Wendy had an idea.

"If we don't have enough rain here in our forest, don't you think that the people in the village are having the same problem?" asked Wendy.

"I'm sure they are having the same problem," answered Olivia. "If you and your friends have walked these long distances and everything you see is brown, then I'm sure the villagers are having their own troubles."

"Do you think it would do any good for us to go talk to them?" asked Wendy.

"I think there would be no harm in talking to them," answered Olivia. "Maybe they know something that we forest animals don't know about."

So that was settled: they decided to visit the villagers.

It was now time for Olivia to go to sleep, so they made a plan. She would sleep during the day, and Wendy would go into the village and find out if the villagers would talk to the forest animals about the water problem. If the villagers agreed, then Wendy would come back in the evening to tell Olivia.

Wendy thanked Olivia and left. Olivia washed up the tea things and then went to sleep.

Wendy went back to the pine tree: she wanted to find out if anyone wanted to go with her into the village. She thought it would be better if there was more than one forest animal that went into the village to talk to the people.

She knocked on Sebastian's door, and then on Wally's door, and then on William's door. They all went to Wendy's house so that she could explain what she and Olivia had talked about.

"So what do we need to do first?" asked Sebastian.

"We just need to go into the village and talk to some of the people and see what they have to say," answered Wendy.

"Maybe they already know what to do about the water problem," said Wally.

"I don't know," said Wendy, "but I'm sure they will not mind talking to us."

So the four friends left the old pine tree and were soon at the edge of the forest. They went into the village where they found a few people standing and talking in front of a shop.

"Excuse us," said Wendy, "but we were wondering if we could talk to any of the villagers who might know what to do about the water problem."

One of the villagers said, "Yes. We are having a meeting tonight in the church to try to figure out what can be done."

"May we join you?" asked Sebastian.

"Of course you may," answered the villager.

Success!

The four friends went back to the old pine tree. Wendy waited a while before she went over to Olivia's house to tell her the good news.

The villagers knew so much more than the forest animals about certain things. Maybe there was hope for an answer to the water problem after all!

CHAPTER SEVEN

The Meeting

Wendy had asked Olivia to join them, so now there were five forest animals who were going to the village. Wendy, Wally, William, and Sebastian were waiting at the bottom of the old pine tree when Olivia arrived.

The village was quite small with mostly just houses and a few shops, so the people used the church as a place to meet. There were regular monthly meetings, and then sometimes there were extra meetings if there was a problem in the village that needed to be fixed.

When the forest animals went into the church, the leader of the village meeting welcomed them. He invited them to sit up close to the front of the church so that everyone could easily hear each other.

The people had talked about other things before the forest animals arrived. But now it was time to talk about the water problem.

"We are happy that you are joining our little meeting," said the leader to the animals. "I'm sure you and all of the other forest animals are just as worried as we are about the water problem."

A few more people from the village were coming in, so the leader waited a few minutes until everyone was seated. Then he said to the animals, "Oh, and one other thing: please feel free to ask questions if you need to."

Olivia thanked him and then asked, "Have you talked about this problem before

in earlier meetings?"

"Oh, yes," answered the leader. "We have been talking about the water problem for a long time now."

"May we ask if you have had any ideas?" asked Olivia. She was the oldest and wisest of the five forest animals, so the other four had asked her to do the speaking at the meeting.

"So far we have not had any ideas that we think will work for us," answered the leader. "We can have water brought here by truck, but that is very expensive. Do you have any ideas?"

Olivia explained to the people what the four friends had tried so far.

"These four friends have had a few ideas," said Olivia. "They found a pond on their map, but when they got there, the pond was dry just like Big River and Raging River."

"Yes," said the leader. "We knew about that pond, but, as you've said, it's dry so that can not help us."

"We also had an idea about using a wooden channel to bring water from the waterfall on Mount Evergreen," said Olivia. "But there is no water flowing over there at this time."

"That's amazing," said the leader. "We've never known that waterfall to stop flowing. So this is more serious than we thought."

No one spoke for a while: everyone was thinking hard and trying to come up with another idea.

"Are there people who use special equipment to look for underground water?" asked Olivia.

"Good question," said the leader. "Yes, there are people who look for underground water. Last week, we had someone here to test our area for underground water. He said there is underground water, but right now it is so deep underground that it would be very expensive to bring water up from underground."

"That's interesting," said Olivia. "Have you had any other ideas?"

"No," answered the leader. "We think we just have to wait until the weather changes and some rain clouds come here to our area."

Just then, there was a loud sound in the distance.

"That sounded like thunder," said the leader. "Strange: we didn't see any clouds as we were coming into the church."

One of the people from the village asked about the beavers, and the leader said, "They are gone. There was so little water in their lake that they had to move."

"Does anyone know where they went?" asked Olivia.

"No one knows for sure," answered the leader. "But there was a rumour that the beavers decided to travel south of our area to look for another place to build a dam and make another lake."

"I guess it doesn't really matter where they went," said Olivia. "If they went so far away that they left our area, even if they did find water, it would not help us because it would be too far away."

"You are right," said the leader. "We either need to have some rain, or come up with an idea that fixes the problem close to our area."

No one spoke for a while. Then Olivia asked, "Have you talked about the danger of fires? Right now all of the plants are so brown and dry that I think a fire could easily start."

"Yes," answered the leader. "We have talked about the danger of fires and what to do about them. We've asked people not to make any kind of fires outside. We've asked campers not to make any campfires; that would be very dangerous. And we've put up signs that tell people to be careful."

"I'm really glad to hear that you've done this," said Olivia. "I've heard that many forest fires are started by people who are not careful."

"Thank you," said the leader. "We've tried to think of ways to have more water, and we've also talked about asking everyone to be careful. But other than that, we don't know what else we can do except to keep our fingers crossed and hope for some rain to come."

There didn't seem to be anything else to talk about. "We thank you for coming to our meeting," said the leader to the forest animals. "If anyone thinks of another idea, please let us know."

"Yes," said Olivia. "We'll make sure to tell you right away."

"We usually have a few snacks after our meeting," said the leader. "Would you like to join us?"

All of the forest animals were happy to be invited for some snacks and thanked the leader.

As they all moved towards the back of the church where the snacks sat on a table, the people and the animals all looked out of the back door. In the distance they saw a bright light.

There was a forest fire!

CHAPTER EIGHT

The Bright Sky

The people and the forest animals stood quite still on the steps outside of the church. They were in shock at what they were seeing.

"I've never seen anything like it," said the leader.

"What should we do?" asked one of the people from the village. "We need to stop it before it comes here to our village."

Olivia cleared her throat. She wanted to remind the people that there were other reasons to stop the fire as quickly as possible.

"Yes," said the leader. "We must not forget our guests here. There are many creatures living in the forest, so we must try to stop the fire as soon as we can."

No one needed to ask what had started the fire; it had to have been the lightning that had happened while they were all inside of the church. They had heard the thunder but had not seen the lightning because they were inside.

"We all need to grab our buckets and shovels," said the leader. "If there is some water left in small pools in Big River, we can use that. We can use our shovels to dig into the earth and throw ground on the fire."

"What can we do to help?" Olivia asked the leader.

"You can fly over the area and then come back to tell us exactly where the fire is," answered the leader.

The people ran towards their houses to get as many buckets and shovels as they could find. Olivia led Wendy, Wally, and William for their flight over the forest. Sebastian, of course, could not fly, so he waited for the people and then went with them.

The people were now coming out of their houses carrying their buckets and shovels. The leader of the meeting was still in charge, so everyone followed him. They left their village and ran towards the forest and the dangerous fire. Sebastian ran along with them.

As they were running the leader said, "I think we are in luck: I think right now the fire is only in one area of the forest. It has not yet spread over a large area."

The people of the village as well as Sebastian were glad to hear this. But Sebastian was scared: they seemed to be running in the direction of the old pine tree!

By now Olivia and the three other birds were flying high over the forest. They could easily see where the forest fire was: it was not at the old pine tree.

But it was not far away from it!

The four of them could not help worrying about the old pine tree. It was so special to the forest and to all of the animals who lived there. And not just the animals living in the tree; it was the most important tree in the forest and all of the forest animals used the tree as a place to rest and as a meeting place.

They could never replace the old pine tree if something bad happened to it.

It was also an important tree because the people from the village and the animals all came together to decorate the old pine tree at Christmas time. So if something happened to it, the forest animals as well as the people from the village would miss it very much.

Olivia and the three other birds continued to fly towards Big River. Olivia wanted to see if there was any water left in the river. There were a couple of pools of water here and there, but not very much. Then the four birds turned around and flew back towards the village. They didn't need to fly very far because the people and Sebastian were already deep inside the forest.

Olivia flew above the people and told them where the fire was.

"The lightning struck a tall dry tree about halfway between the old pine tree and Big River," she told them as they continued to run. "The fire is only burning in that one area."

"That's good to hear," said the leader as he continued to run. "Is there any water that we can use from Big River?"

As she and the other three birds flew above the leader, the other people from the village, and little Sebastian, Olivia answered, "There are some small pools of water here and there, but not very much."

"Well," said the leader. "Any little bit will help. But we'll start with the shovels and dirt first."

Olivia and the three other birds continued to fly just above the heads of the people and Sebastian as they ran towards the fire. Their path now crossed right in front of the old pine tree. No one spoke: they all looked at the special tree and hoped that they would be able to save it.

Now they had passed the tree and were getting closer to the fire. They put down their buckets and started to use their shovels. Sebastian and the four birds were not able to help with these heavy tools, so they stood nearby and watched.

The people dug in the earth below the layers of dry, dead leaves. It was not easy work; there were a lot of leaves on the floor of the forest!

But the people were doing a good job. Every time they threw a shovel full of ground on the fire, they were able to make it just a little smaller.

By now, other forest animals had joined Olivia, the three other birds, and Sebastian. No one spoke; they all just stood there watching the people working hard to put out the fire.

All of the people and all of the animals were so busy looking at the fire on the ground that no one had looked up at the sky. Huge, dark storm clouds were now moving into the area.

The people had almost finished putting out the fire when there was a huge clap of thunder; the lightning hit another tree not far away.

A new fire started!

© comodo777 | Adobe Stock

CHAPTER NINE

Buckets!

"Oh no!" shouted Olivia.

The people grabbed their shovels and started to work on this new fire. But it seemed so much bigger than the other fire, and it seemed to be moving very fast across the floor of the forest.

"I don't think this is working this time," said one of the people from the village.

The leader agreed: "You're right: we must have water."

But how could they get water from Big River? And was there enough water in Big River to help put out the fire?

Suddenly Olivia shouted, "We'll help."

"How?" asked the leader.

"We'll gather as many animals as we can and bring water from Big River," she answered.

"Will there be enough water to help?" asked the leader.

"All we can do is to try and see what happens," answered Olivia.

While the people continued to use their shovels to throw ground on the fire, Olivia and her four friends went as quickly as they could to places all around the forest

looking for their other animal friends.

When they came back to get the buckets, there were quite a few animals! The people of the village were amazed at what they saw.

There was Olivia the Owl, Wendy the Warbler, Wally the Woodlark, William the Woodpecker, Sebastian the Squirrel, Cherry the Chipmunk, Oscar the Otter, Daisy the Deer, Ronald the Rabbit, Faith the Fox, Steven the Snake, Megan the Mink, and many other animals.

The people were still using their shovels as they watched the animals pick up the buckets and run towards Big River. Olivia led the way because she knew where they could find the most water in the river.

All of the animals dropped their buckets next to the largest pool in the nearly dry Big River. Then they formed a line from the river back towards the area where the fire was.

Oscar the Otter was an Olympic swimmer and quite strong, so he was in charge of dipping the empty buckets into the pool of water and handing the bucket to the next animal. Each animal got the bucket with water in it and passed it on to the next animal.

Soon there was a line of animals passing buckets of water from the pool at Big River the whole way to where the fire was. Sebastian was at the end of the line, closest to the fire. After he threw the water from the bucket on to the fire, he passed the empty bucket to Olivia who was the next to last animal in the line.

So buckets full of water were passed from one animal to the next from the river to the fire, and then the empty buckets were passed by the animals back to the river where Oscar filled each empty bucket with water.

While the animals were on one side of the fire, the side facing the river, the people from the village were on the other side of the fire, the side facing the village, and were still using their shovels. They were trying to work as quickly as they could to use ground to put out the fire.

All of the people and all of the animals were working so hard and so fast that no one noticed that the fire was moving closer and closer to the old pine tree!

The fire was now out of control. The storm clouds were the problem: they were making it very windy in the forest, and the wind made the fire move very quickly.

So now there was the fire and the wind making the fire worse.

The leader of the people said, "I don't think we can do this much longer. The fire is getting bigger instead of smaller."

Olivia was on the other side of the fire, and she was thinking the same thing. "I think the wind is making this fire too big for us. Even with the shovels of ground and the buckets of water, the fire is spreading too quickly for us."

It was then that she saw how close the fire was moving towards the old pine tree. They must save the old pine tree! But how?

She flew around the fire so that she could talk to the leader of the people.

"Do you see how close the fire is getting to the old pine tree?" she asked him.

He looked up from his shoveling and said, "Oh, no!"

"What can we do?" Olivia asked the leader.

"We must do two things," he said. "First of all, we will use our shovels to build up a wall of ground around the old pine tree."

"Good idea," said Olivia. "And the second thing?"

"You animals must use the water and the buckets to make the needles of the old pine tree wet," he answered.

"Why is that?" asked Olivia.

"Because we might be able to control the fire on the ground near the tree," answered the leader. "But the fire can jump easily from one tree to the next. So we must make sure the old pine tree is wet."

"I understand," said Olivia.

So now the plan changed: saving the old pine tree became the most important job.

The people grabbed their shovels and started to make a wall of ground in a circle around the bottom of the old pine tree. This way, the fire would stop on the floor of the forest before it reached the old pine tree.

At the same time, the animals were carrying buckets of water to the old pine tree. Some of them threw water on its bottom branches. The birds carried buckets of water to the top branches, and soon, the whole tree was wet.

But it wasn't enough. The fire was now quite close to the old pine tree. The people grabbed their shovels and ran. The animals grabbed their buckets and ran.

The old pine tree was now on fire!

CHAPTER TEN

Little Green Plants

Wendy was the first to feel it. It was a drop of water. It was rain! The rain started slowly and gently, but soon it began to rain harder and harder. The clouds were finally doing their job!

Everyone was so happy that they started to clap!

The first thing that happened was that the small fire on the old pine tree was stopped by the strong rain. This made all of the forest animals and the people from the village very happy.

"I've never seen it rain like this before," said Wendy.

"I wish I had closed my windows," said Wally, as he flew up to his house to close a few of his windows.

The next thing that happened was that the rest of the forest fire was put out by the heavy rain. Every little bit of fire here and there was now gone.

"No more shovels!" shouted the people from the village.

"No more buckets of water!" shouted the forest animals.

Everyone was happy that the rain had come. It had put out the forest fire, and now Big River and Raging River would be full of water once again. And there

would be water for the pond and for the waterfall on Mount Evergreen.

So why was there a little sadness in the forest?

All of the people from the village and all the animals from the forest were now under the old pine tree so that they could get out of the heavy rain. From here, they looked out over the forest.

There was sadness because there were large areas of the forest that were now black because of the fire. Everyone stood under the tree and looked out from under the branches of the old pine tree. The forest was not beautiful any longer.

***

It was Wendy again who first saw it. She was on her way from the old pine tree to visit Olivia. And there, in the black part of the forest, she saw something green.

She went over to see what it was. It was a tiny bud: it was a new plant that was coming up from the area where the fire had turned everything black.

She looked over to her right and saw something else that was green. She went over and was happy to see another little plant coming up from the black floor of the forest.

Wendy was so excited she went to Olivia's as fast as she could. Olivia had invited Wendy over to her house: it was evening so Olivia wasn't sleeping and she had not yet gone out for her night time activities.

Wendy knocked on Olivia's door. Olivia opened the door, and Wendy was so excited she could hardly speak.

"Sit down, Wendy, and take a big deep breath," said Olivia.

Finally Wendy could talk. She said, "You're never going to believe what I just saw."

"What was it?" asked Olivia.

"I saw a couple of new little green plants growing up in the black part of the forest!" she answered.

"That's great!" said Olivia. "I wondered when we would start to see some green in the black."

"You knew there would be plants?" Wendy asked Olivia.

"Oh yes," answered Olivia. "Every time after a forest fire, new plants start to shoot up from the floor of the forest."

"Even if it's black?" asked Wendy.

"Yes," answered Olivia. "Under the black there is ground, and seeds, and with some rain, the new plants start to replace the old plants that were burned from the fire.

"Let's tell everybody about it, okay?" asked Wendy.

"Okay," answered Olivia. She could see how happy and excited Wendy was, and how much she wanted to share this with the other forest animals.

First they went to the old pine tree to tell Wally, William, and Sebastian. They wanted to see what Wendy was talking about, so Wendy led all of them over to the new little green plants in the black part of the forest.

Soon other animals joined them. They all looked around and saw many other little plants coming up. It was almost like a new plant popped up every other minute, there were so many of them!

Then Wendy had an idea: "Let's go tell the people in the village. They will want to know, right?"

So it happened that a large group of forest animals entered the village. All the people came out of their houses and shops to find out what was happening. They were surprised to hear about the new little green plants.

"Come and see!" said Wendy. "Join us and we'll show you."

So all the people of the village followed the forest animals into the black part of the forest. And here they pointed out all the new little green plants.

"This is amazing!" said the leader of the people. "It's so soon after the fire to see these little green plants."

They were standing not too far away from the old pine tree.

"I'm so glad the rain came just in time to save the old pine tree," said the leader. Everyone agreed with him.

Every day after that, more and more little green plants popped up. Some of these little green plants were trees, some were shrubs, and some were flowers.

The plants continued to grow until there was no more black left: everything was green.

But that was not the only good news. The beavers had returned! When water started to flow out of Big Spring and make Big River big again, the beavers came back to their homes which were still there in the lake.

And there was water in the pond that the four friends had found. And the waterfall was flowing again on Mount Evergreen.

All the people from the village and all of the animals from the forest kept their fingers crossed that there would always be enough rain, especially for the old pine tree!

The End

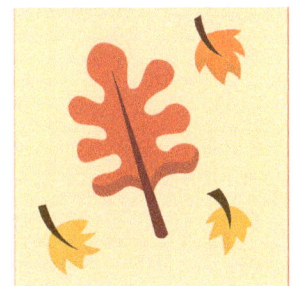

© comodo777 | Adobe Stock

THE AUTHOR

Edward Alan Kurtz

Edward is an American writer. He specializes in writing works of fiction and non-fiction for children, as well as travel books and articles.

Ed was born in Pennsylvania and completed several university degrees.

He lived for many years in Honolulu, Hawaii, and now lives and writes in Thailand.

Previous books with Stergiou publications:

- Max and The Map
- Christmas in the Forest
- Springtime in the Forest
- Summertime in the Forest

www.ingramcontent.com/pod-product-compliance
Lightning Source LLC
Chambersburg PA
CBHW042036100526
44587CB00030B/4453